*To my brother Lucky*
*Thank you &*
*I hope you fi[nd]*
*these pages ..... you and your*
*family.*

*Forever your sister*
*Reina Miranda*
*AKA Red Clay Woman*
*12/14*

# Tree Of Life
# The Roots Of My Journey

*a collection of poetry by*

REINA MIRANDA

Tree Of Life - The Roots Of My Journey

Copyright © 2014 by Reina M. Miranda

All rights reserved. Manufactured in the United States. No part of this book can be used or reproduced in any manner without written permission except in the case of brief quotations embodied in critical articles and reviews. For information, contact redclaywoman304@gmail.com

Published by Cats Meow Media Press

Tree of Life: Roots of My Journey / [edited by] R. Borrero and R. Miranda– 1st ed.

ISBN - 978-0692245170

Cover Art by Reina M. Miranda

# CONTENTS

The Love Of A Granddaughter
1
You Ask Me
3
My Life In Santo Domingo
5
How Dare You
7
Taino Love 2
9
Life- Funny As It Seems
11
My Garden
13
Lost In My Thoughts
15
Need 17
La Taina
19
My Transformation

21
All Women
23
What A Surprise
25
Confliction
27
Cemi Island
29
Despierta Mi Gente
30
Miracle
32
Respect
34
Self__36
Taino Four Elements
38
Wounds
40
Writer's Block
42
You've Got It All
44
Addiction

46
Sacred Waters
48
Rain = Cry
50
Sidewalk Memories
52
Goodbye To Lies
54
What?
56
Taino Past and Present
58
The Days Of Old
60
Games People Play
62
Homenaje Spoken
64
Glossary Of Taino Words
67
Acknowledgements
68
About The Author
72

**Taino Beauty**

My grandmother passed into the Koaibei (the Spirit World) in (2006). She was 95 years old and I know that she is always looking out for me.

She continues to be a major source of inspiration for me. She was the one who taught me about survival and about taking time to appreciate the world around me. She is one of the reasons I am the woman I am today.

I dedicate this book to her memory because she is my muse. I Love you Abuelita Erani Tavera.

There are many others I would like to thank for their support and love – too many indeed but I want to thank to my art teacher Aguilar Marrero, my …., and my friend and brother Kasike Múkaro Agueibana – Roberto Borrero. Múkaro is always there for his people and I consider him one of the great contemporary Taíno leaders of our time.

# TREE OF LIFE

### *The Love Of A Granddaughter*

Like the mountains of *Kiskeia*...
The love I have is great and strong...

Like the mountains of *Kiskeia*...
The love she had remains like a sweet, sweet song...

We shared a life that no one can have...
I see her smile and I am not sad...

Stories of her youth allowed me to live her past...
95 years young seemed to fly by so fast...

She is me and I am her...

I will miss her soft touch, that is what I yearn.
She took the time to teach and I wanted to learn...

I wanted to learn about the mountains and the sea...
I wanted to learn what made me...

She is me and I am her...

Abuela, thank you for sharing your life's journey and teachings...
Abuela, you are my rock, the sun that shines,
I promise I will keep reaching...

Like the mountains of *Kiskeia*...
I hold you close to my heart in times of strife...
I know that you here beside me as I walk the road

called life.

>Like the mountains of *Kiskeia*...
>The love I have is great and strong...

>Like the mountains of *Kiskeia*...
>The love she had remains like a sweet, sweet song...

## *You Ask Me*

You ask me who am I?

I tell you that I am *Anacaona*... Taíno Kasike of Kiskeia la bella...

Again you ask me who am I? I tell you that I am mother of those seeking refuge. I am the Earth Mountain and the soft grass where children rest their weary heads. I am the birthplace of all those who ask questions and want to know where it is they came from...

My name is *Atabei* – Life Giver - Earth Mother...

My name is *Kiskeia*... I am the birthplace of the Taíno. The good ones... I am the sacred cave... For those who choose to understand, my name symbolizes the ancestral heart... And I can feel the hurt of my children and land.

When you fall, I am there to pick you up.

When you bleed, I can heal your wounds.

When you need shelter, I am there to cover you from the cold and rain.

Who am I?
There is no need to ask child for I am you, you and you.

The people of yesterday, today, and tomorrow - the

ancestry of three – a sacred number... And an island in the turquoise blue Caribbean sea.

The Taíno, African and Spaniard are the bloodlines that in the end were made to be. I am you, you, and you.... And you are me.

Uniquely different with a heart that sets us apart...
Now we shout at the top of our lungs that we still exist and the revolution is about to start... Its time to acknowledge and time to see,
Like our mother we give of ourselves but are mistreated and continue to be...

We have been forgotten, used, and abused.... Now only a few left to plant the seeds... We are not a plague or disease... We are peace and love and it's time to seize the day... We are on our way... Back to the start... Back to the heart...

So who are you to question your mother? Is this how you were raised? Tu cres que tú te manda? Por favor...

Tell me how can you stand there and still wonder. I gave of myself to make sure that our story lives on in you. Can't you hear it in the thunder?

Hispaniola or Dominican Republic - my name has been changed but I remain your *bohio* --- I am called *Kiskeia* with a capital K.

## *My Life In Santo Domingo*

My life was so simple living in the capital of Santo Domingo... In a small town, growing ever so peaceful, it was really so beautiful that I could never frown.

You see I am a young woman born of four... The only female child along with my three brothers whom I showed appreciation and I adored.

My mother sent me to my godmother's to be raised in the tradition and culture,
to live with a family who knew me well and taught me how to be a true woman.
Left my home never to see my mother and brothers until the time was right.

Growing up in this town called Santiago where I never had the need to fight.
My education began – I was doing things – preparing for my journey,
Unaware that there was a suitor waiting... We started of as friends and nothing more... He made me smile and laugh - it was like he opened a door....

He loved me honorably from afar and told his family that he would have me as his wife, I was living at my godmother's home for the better part of my life.
He mustered the courage to ask my hand in marriage,

My mother and godmother gave us their ultimate blessing.

I was dressed all in white unable to see him until the days of all days, walking into a room for our beloved wedding day... What more can I say...

You see we did not get married in a church but in a courthouse that was our first day - he was now my spouse.

He made me a home, worked day and night trying to make us a new life... I was such a loving wife...

Then came the day came for him to leave for work on the next island... He left for Puerto Rico and as a shoemaker he was saving his pennies...

I stayed behind to doing the same - saving and saving... Some people thought we were playing games.... I always thought that was a shame... When my husband finally got to the states – everything was working out --- we began to plan for our family...

He sent for me... We were reunited at last... We worked and worked until we finally had our very first apartment.... Working to attain that special dream... trying to reach that place of contentment... We had our ups and downs of course but there is no resentment...

And after 51 years of marriage I am happy to say we have four wonderful children and four grandchildren... the sacrifices and hard work was well worth it – there were even times to play...

I have come a long way from my simple life in the capital of Santo Domingo...

## *How Dare You*

How dare you rape, pillage and destroy our lands? How dare you destroy our beautiful fields with your cold heart, mind, and hands?

How dare you bring plagues unknown to us... Plagues – your cruel gifts that almost killed us all... yes, we struggled but we did not fall...

Our skin is different... You are white and we are brown. Yet we bleed the same... Are we not relatives? Our minds are different... Close to the earth we remain... This is the place of our birth... We are like islands in the sea...

Our mother taught us to be peaceful, sweet, tender, and proud.
However, you gave us poisons that covered these lands in a dark, dark shroud.

How dare you think that we are the ignorant ones when you came to us simply by accident... You were lost and we found you... You are still lost...

We have something that is real – Taíno love and the universe above...

Our spirits live on, the road is long - everyone knows that Taíno are strong.

Okama! Oye! Taíno raise your makanas in hand... It is now time to take back the spirit of our land and make a stand. Taíno are everywhere and we shall rise from the ashes and the sands...

Our ancestors need us to spread the seed... Through our culture, our love, our deeds... How dare you say that we do not exist... How dare you think that we all died... Our children and their children keep our spirits alive.

*Guakia* Taíno (We are Taíno)! *Guakia Yaha* (We are Here)!

## *Taino Love 2*

"Taíno Love 2"

This painting is an homage to my teacher Aguilar Marrero.
The concept is inspired by Aguilar's original painting "Taíno Love", however this one is from a Taíno women's point of view.

Original size: 16x20 (acrylic and watercolors

pencils)

## *Life- Funny As It Seems*

Funny as it seems life brought me something so honest and true...

Funny as it seems that it came to me at the right time too...

You see I lived my life to appease others with the gifts bestowed to me, not able to feel the love so it could be set free.

Now I'm remembering what was taught --- life's lessons that I took for granted...
Taking things as it should --- remember those lessons --- re-vamping...

The feelings that kept me in a box – in a cage like an animal – they are trying to escape... Like a lioness searching for her prey to feed her King so he can announce in a great shout that he still exists and he is the King...

Everyone knows that the pride of a woman is her self-worth – that is her triumph, all the things she does is most surely self-reliance...

I must remember why my ancestors fought for women... Women were held in the highest regard...I am the modern day Taíno Warrior... I am not weak but steadfast as an armed palace guard...

You see I am not a footstool for those to rest their feet... I am not a sore loser or one who will admit defeat...

I am that strong Taíno Woman for all to see... My story will live on beyond the pages in history... I will be there to help some find that story, that lineage, the glue of life that binds.

I do not feel the need to settle... Cause I know that I will reach the finish line to earn my *guanin* gold medal... I will not let myself down because others want me to quit... Damn people, if the glove doesn't fit then you must acquit...

Looking back I have come to see what is in front of me - a warrior, a mother, a lover, a sister and friend... She is me and I am here with a sacred duty... Here to defend... Defend my family with such honor and pride --- this is what our ancestors did before they died.... They died.

To those in *Koaibei* – the spirit world - I say thank you for the wake up call --- I see the big picture...I am a one of the ancient ones and I am your sister... You see I almost forgot the most important lessons of all --- Always put your best foot forward cause divided we fall...

Funny as it seems it took me this long to get it right --- I do not think I will be regressing...

Funny as it seems life is constantly giving me a new lesson.

## *My Garden*

My garden looks ever so lovely...

There is a beautiful flower in my garden.
What makes this one so special? Is it the fragrance that this flower has released?
Is this fragrance better than the rest? Is it the petals, the colors...?

What a special flower – it really stands out.
Well, let me take a closer look and take it in, wow...
I just noticed something a little different, a little strange.
How unique - this special flower grew another right next to it on the same stem.
What a miracle of life.

I can just sit here admiring this flower instead of plucking it from the ground.
I will nurture it and keep it watered so it can grow bigger and more beautiful.
I will pull out all of the weeds to ensure its safety.

As I begin to walk away after a day of tending my garden, I started to think – wow, that flower reminded me of us.

A couple that grew from feelings elated; we are a fragrance twice as nice.
Just as I see that special flower in my garden, I envision our future...
We are standing side by side holding each other

tight...

I hope you understand that the love I have for you. You will constantly hear it and I hope it will never make you feel blue.

Papi, come here and see our love as a garden... do not let it whiter my dear.

'Cause you are my unique flower, I'll make sure that you're safe and secure.

Seeking a future --- hoping all our dreams will be fulfilled...
Dreams of brighter days that will come... We need that sunlight...

I will always be there to pull out the weeds...

Seeking a future --- hoping all our dreams will be fulfilled...
Dreams of brighter days that will come... We need that sunlight...

Remember that cold of winter can keep us dormant for a while... Nevertheless, it always gets warmer and we will emerge lovelier and stronger than before.

So let me get back to my garden... it represents the love we have and will continue to have... It will grow and I am ready for the weeds... I will be there for you and give you everything you need.

My garden looks ever so lovely.

## Lost In My Thoughts

I am lost in my thoughts, lost in emotions that cannot be fought…

These feelings are so good… So overwhelming; I can feel my heart beating faster as its swelling…

What is wrong with me? What is going on? What can I do?

Can this be it? Is this legit? We really do fit? Damn, Boo.

We are like a glove and hand --- Relaxin', chillin', and listening to the sweet soft music of some smooth R&B band...

In anticipation, my imagination and my thoughts are taking me to a whole new world – a different time --- a different place… I am hopin', prayin', dreamin' for our encounter – our divine face-to-face.

Like fine wine and sunsets -- you always manage to make me laugh and smile…

Oh baby, you – me --- who knew this is what I needed all the while…

I feel your essence flowing deep, deep in my veins…
This feeling -- this love -- is reaching deep, deep in my brain…

Yes, my love you are my sweetest juicy strawberry...
I am the melted chocolate for you to dip in so let us get ready...

This sweet sensation is all that I crave and now I all want to do is misbehave...

Waiting for you is taking far too long – it's like that that smooth R&B singer writing that perfect song...

We have something that so special, so pure and unique...

Feelings so strong making us drop to our knees... Feelings so strong we can finally be free...

Let us take this slow and cherish what we have,
Because this is the kind of love that can never go bad...

I am lost in my thoughts, lost in emotions that cannot be fought...

I am lost in my thoughts, lost in the passion for it is you that I've sought.

## Need

Why do some feel the need to tell me what I can do?
Why is it that I still feel the need to prove myself?
Well, it is what it is. If they still do not know it is their loss.

Am I the only one thinking that I am going crazy?
Are those who I call my friends thinking that I am trippin'?
Is my family trying to keep me down?

Internal inquiry... questions... More questions keeping me up at night... long nights... Always analyzing what has been done all around.
Listening to rumors and *indirectos* --- what I can or cannot do.

Aye dios... What is the use?

Am I a trained dog? Waiting for a damn treat?
Why it is that some folks feel the need to belittle me?
Why smile in my face and chat nasty about me behind my back?

Hold up --- Why am I letting this get to me?

Honestly -- I am better than that. Let us cut out all the lies and shift through the nonsense... Cause it seems a lot of folks say they love to see you on your way up but they really celebrate when you hit rock bottom... It is like what Biz Markie said, "Everyone catches the Vapors" never truly working hard to make that paper or even plant that seed.

No one really knows what I have been through – what I am going through...
Constantly following those damn rules that make me look like a damn fool...

What is the point? Are they part of the solution or of the problem?

You know what --- I could care less about what is being said and I do not need to know... I have all my goals set.... I know what I need... I am about to jet.

No more living in this bloody fish bowl straining to see who is going to feed me...

No more jumping through hoops like some sort of circus animal trying to get a treat for some applause...

Like James Dean I am that true rebel without a cause...

So here is my decision - let me dust the dirt off my shoulders and kick it nice.
'Cause I know that I'm in for the biggest fight that anyone can envision...

This is the fight of my life and I know what I need...

## La Taína

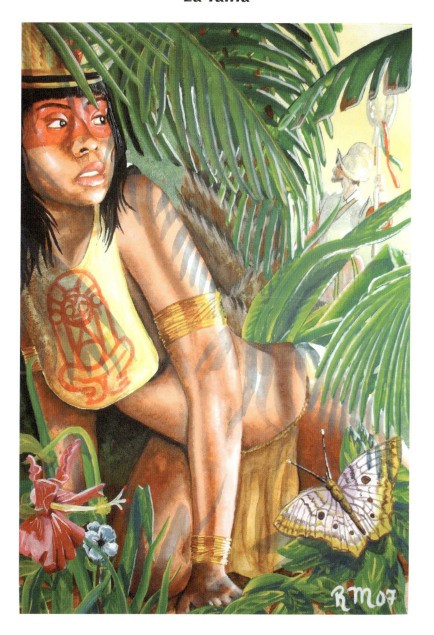

"La Taína"

This painting was displayed at the American Museum of Natural History in New York during a special public program entitled "Living in America: The Allure of Gold" and at United Nations Headquarters as part of the exhibition "In Celebration of Indigenous Peoples during the Permanent Forum on Indigenous Issues from May 2007 to September 2007. In this painting, different interpretations emerge depending on your point of view. Every one has their own story to tell. *La Taína* is one of my most popular works.

Original size: 16x20 (acrylic and watercolors pencils)

## My Transformation

Let me begin by issuing this special declaration - The world around us is in constant transformation.... I am a source of this information...

I just do not transform, I evolve into something so much more.

The beauty within as well as the outward... To be one with *Atabei* – the Life Giver - to be close to her womb... to hear her secrets...

Questions I have... Questions... Is everyone doing what is needed?

Now hear this... Now hear this... Can someone tell me how others transform?
Are these transformations the results of vices forlorn?

Questions I have... Questions... Do these transformations achieve the results desired? Are these results beauty shared for all to see? Do they take one higher?

Transformation is not just a statement or a minor verb... It is a proclamation of the mind, body and soul that in the end everyone will hear. The world around us is in constant transformation.... I am a source of this information...

In my transformation I can feel my spirit soar into the heavens like a sacred eagle in flight.... Is this what you feel in your transformation? Will it be better than before?

Questions I have... Questions... Will you remain dormant like a flower in winter? Will you be like a lioness exclaiming her royal and mighty roar?

The world around us is in constant transformation.... I am a source of this information...

## *All Women*

As I walk down the street I happen to notice a person looking at me and it makes me wonder what is it that they really see?

Do they think I am a toy with a sexy body with out of control curves or maybe that I am ugly and look like a like a boy? Well, it does not matter what they see - trust me… trust me…

I can tell you what it is and what I know… I see them when I look in the mirror, I see them as far back as I go… I see all my mothers – those who came before me… Yes I said it --- all of my mothers --- different lifestyles and different faces... Yes, they come from so many places… I see them coming from the Caribbean islands… They are women of *Kiskeia*, *Kuba* y *Boriken* --- las Islas mas bella…

Desde el Caribe --- I see the freedom fighters that stood their sacred ground and fought for my rights through the long hard nights… They fill me with such pride; their sacrifices make it so that no one can ever really hurt me or make me hide…

With strong backs they came… carrying those who could not make it on their own… They traveled many journeys and they walked many roads… Traveling through the thick and thing down the journey roads…

So my friend what you see before you is a warrior, a *kasike*, a queen, a mother, a daughter and a sister.

Damn it y'all is it not obvious that I am every woman - all women...

We are here --- we continue --- we are descended from on high and have ascended from down below... We are the beginning... We are the end... We we gave birth to light so is it any wonder that some choose to admire and delight in the presence and the essence of the universe... Are we not the Mother of Creation?

Damn it y'all is it not obvious that I am every woman...

As I walk down the street I happen to notice a person looking at me and it makes me wonder what is it that they really see?

Well, it does not matter what they see - trust me... I can tell you what it is and what I know... We are warriors; we are blessed with a vision... Making a difference in lives, and making decisions... Maybe they see super models or hard luck cases... Maybe they see each of us uniquely beautiful for we are reflecting ... projecting... The birth of the universe...

Damn it y'all is it not obvious that I am every woman – all women...

## What A Surprise

Wow, what a surprise how things work out,
Damn, something is buggin' me, I'm heated and I want to shout.
Why must things turn out this way?
Must things like this happen on a day like today?

Me - always there for you when you need a friend, when you need bread...
Me - I'm the friend on whose lap you can lay and rest your weary head.
When you cry we both cry... I am and have been there for you as the days go by and by.

You - Can you see past your own goals?
You - Do you value friendship like you value your gold?
What will it take for you to see? Will you ever plant the seed?
I'm talkin' about the seed of friendship that grows into happiness...
But on the other hand are you sowing seeds of regret? Ah but I digress...

There are so many things here for you to learn...
These are things that others are eager for, things that others yearn.
Now the anger I feel is great and true,
This is that cold, dark feeling that makes me blue when I think of you...

Do you value the gifts given to you?
Do you think that others have important views?

There is a saying that stands out in my mind,
The more you change the more things stay the same.

How true are these words? Are these just minor verbs?

Surprise - we live life to receive its' lessons, it is something we all should reckon. Friendship and love are gifts from the Great Creator for us to share...

No one and I mean no one should ever live in despair.

## *Confliction*

Sitting here and thinking about things that are coming, I am forever missing the things that are here... The most important lessons... I am missing the ones I love and hold dear - they are what I truly need, they are what feed me... Feeling conflicted – I am between two worlds – conflicted – and that makes me wonder...

I have loved with all my heart, body and soul, searching for the proper conduit, searching for something that can make me whole. It is not what everyone thinks. No, it is not that I want to replace something with something... something that will just make it all better. It's deeper... deeper... deeper.

I want to be me and nothing more as if I was standing by the ocean and breathing in the shore. Living life to the fullest – isn't that what everyone strives for? Hey, we are told not to look back but I find myself constantly wondering what it is I lack. Am I loving my others more than I love me? Do I love the world that goes on and on as far as I can see? Or is it something close... maybe I don't see...I'm feeling so conflicted that it has me so numb - most times I feel lost, alone and dumb.

Putting others ahead is what I have done all my life. Now I am stricken with grief, loss and discrepancies. Never ever seeing the brightness of the sun, while its keeping me warm and blessing me with such eternal admiration – My focus has turned cloudy - is it my time to leave this equation? Is there is quick repair, a more formal, final declaration...

Why do I consider this a means to an end? Whose heart am I trying to mend? Yours or mine? Yours or mine? Who is it I am trying to find? I'm running in circles conflicted and now the face that I am ashamed of has me looking for guidance.

I am like a runner running from something but can't get away... Rather then confront it and achieve my freedom, I avoid it and stay...

Conflicted - not knowing where to go - here or there... Knowing fully that life is not fair. Why is this happening and why did I allow it? Is there a cure? Is this my test of faith? Will I keep striving to negate?

Should I take that giant leap into the dark, deep waters? I need it to wash away this craziness. Oh to be clean... I desire to make a change -- my children, family, myself --- I need to re-gain. Wanting to be alone is not the answer but I need to take care of me before I can take care of you... you.... Me...

I wonder what will happen when I am gone. Will there be a sweet loving song?

A song about a woman who brought joy, love or even cared? Or will the eulogy highlight the fear and what made me scared. Who is to say whether there will be such a thing? Conflicted, I need to know --- will you remember me?

## *Cemi Island*

"Cemi Island"

This painting depicts my version of a *Cemi*; a three-pointed icon used by the ancient Taíno in their *bohio* (homes) or in the fields, planted like seeds for good harvest. These icons were craved from stone, wood, or bone.
There are many different types of *Cemi*. On this particular one, the way I understand it is that the top is always pointing to the Great Creator.
The front part where it looks like a face, represents those who are living.
The back part represents the spirits of those who have crossed over to *Koaibei*.

Original size: 16x20 (acrylic)

## *Despierta Mi Gente*

Our voices united hit everyone hard - so powerful, so true and full of strength.

My God we were on point even though our words were not of great length... Moved deeply was the way everyone felt... They knew what it was that they were dealt... It hit them hard with so much emotion... It was as if the words were a magic potion... transformation was in motion... Or at least it was in my mind...

In reality, my dream is to see us unite... Instead of doing so however, some amongst us continue to fight. Why is it that we cannot see that this is part of the divide and conquer scheme... Why remain asleep? How long will our people weep? When will our hands as one finally meet? Is it any wonder why it's hard for us to get to our feet? Can't you hear the ancestral drum beats?

They are calling!!! Ancient drums calling... Despierta mi gente!!!

Somos *Borikua, Kiskeiano* y *Kubano. Han han Katu* - so be it - as it is said... We are the people of yesterday, today, and tomorrow.

They are calling!!! Ancient drums calling... Despierta mi gente!!!

Spread the word my sisters and brothers - spread the word. We as one united will be heard. My sisters and brothers we are strong, we have seen too much pain for far too long. The ancestors have blessed us with a vision... Realize it or not we have already begun our march and we will complete the mission.

Continue to stand, to shout and to fight. However you do it - do it with all your might. Our eyes can be open with words once dreamed now spoken...
Despierta mi gente - the spell can broken. Our time is now and the door is open. You know what you need to do – get up, join hands and march through...

Despierta *Boricua, Kiskeiano,* y *Kubano,* for yesterday, for today, and tomorrow.

## *Miracle*

Being the oldest never kept me sober.
I have been through so much and many times I've felt that my life was over...
An ongoing cycle of feeling lonely and blue,
Until the day, I stepped out of that shadow and lit the light anew.

My family never truly made me feel like gold.
I have spent sleepless nights not knowing where I could go truth be told...
You see it took me to marry young to get me out on what I thought was my own,
However, reality hits hard and I still ended up back at my parent's home.

My ex-husband – as you may have guessed – he did not want to work to support me... So I went to work and came home for him to beat me – beat me.
Still lookin' for love - I became pregnant with my oldest son,
As you may have guessed, that man, that bastard told me he was not the one...

That was it – All I could stand - I told him to get out and leave,
That so-called man wanted to break my spirit; he wanted to see me bleed...
To him I was a horse and he needed to show me he was the master...
That is how it went – I was movin' slowly but the world was movin' faster...

When I felt my son's first movement I truly felt love,
He was my little miracle – an angel from above…
A renewed strength I knew that he would help me to venture on.
Now that hurt – that hate – it seemed like it all was gone…

You see my life was in chaos until I saw what needed to be seen,
The looks on my son's face - the one who loves and needs me.
He is my little miracle, my little angel, my little dream…

## *Respect*

You say you want respect but you do not give the same.
Respect is something that you need to earn, something you need to gain.
You belittle, disparage and discourage those that are around,
Unaware that you are standing on very unstable ground…

Respect is not just a word; it is a way of life – it's that one song that needs to be heard.

It's a feeling – a knowing that someone can help create,
Instead, you choose to complain and or simply negate…
Making things more difficult - nothing gets its proper place.
Instead, you argue with me in an endless face-to-face,

I never claim to be perfect in uncertain terms;
I as said my friend respect is something that needs to be earned.
To gain trust is what everyone needs; with words and deeds we plant seeds.

Respect is not just a word; it is a way of life - it's that one song that needs to be heard.

You – me - we struggle amongst ourselves when we could be as one,

Guilty of the same - yes I must admit but thy will can be done.
As respect is something that we all desire,
please just tell me there is a way to put out this fire.

Tell me is there a solution to this minor setback.
Or is this another old coat that we hang on the rack?
Is there a resolution – a way we can agree? Is there a potion that can set us free?

Respect is not just a word; it is a way of life - it's that one song that needs to be heard.

These are some questions that make me often wonder; they are not the dreams of idle slumber. Respect is a gift of mutual trust and it is within our grasp,
Take it within your soul and work hard so it last.

Respect is not just a word; it is a way of life - it's that one song that needs to be heard.

## *Self*

Constantly trying to prove my self worth...
I am tryin' so hard but it continues to hurt,

Constantly trying to just get ahead,
But being so tired I got to wishing I were dead.

I was thinking death seemed the only way out of this hell;
So I climbed to the highest roof top and began to yell.

Why must you all make me scream? Over and over like a bad dream.

Can't you all just let me be? Don't you see what you are doing to me?

Screaming at the top of my lungs - let's see if I can take the plunge.
It's just a step further --- the edge ---- and then slight lunge...

Wait a minute. What am I doing here? Is this the end of my rope?
Hold up, Hold up. Why I am acting like such a big, cry-baby dope.

Forget this madness - I am doing me and just me,
I can be the love that inspires – I can be what I want to be.

Man, some people are just jealous with nothing

better to do
    Than look down, put down, they just want to get inside of you

    Well, they can all kiss my backside. I am moving on, I got nothin' to hide
    And by the way, work is what is and I am not its slave. I will not allow it to put me in an early grave.

    I am here now and I am here to stay, my train is rolling, so stay out of my way.

# *Taino Four Elements*

"Taíno Four Elements"

In this painting, I used my face because what better model than a *Taína* like me!

Anyway, at the top of the image is the Caribbean Sea and the islands of *Kuba, Kiskeia, Hamaika* and *Boriken*.

In the middle are three Cemi (spirits), from left to right the Moon Goddess, the Sun Spirit and the Bleeding Earth Mother – *Itiba Kahubaba*. In addition, on the bottom is a *bohio* (a home) with cassava (*Yuka*) bread being prepared. In each one of the faces, I used the symbols for the elements of Wind, Water, Fire and Earth. Without these elements we cannot exist.

I feel this portrays the deep love I have for my Taíno culture and my ancestors and the love they have for me.

Original size: 20x30 (acrylic and watercolor pencils)

## *Wounds*

It's said that with time the wounds will heal.
How true is that?
Does anyone have the answer to that question?
Others say, "Me and time with any two will do",
What is a person truly trying to do?

Lost and confused with scars that I have acquired throughout this life. Thinking maybe I should give up and let others walk all over me again.

Alternatively I wonder, should I continue to fight?

My past has me in a mental prison, things I have done are coming back to haunt and torture me into thinking that I can never change.

Promises I have made to myself - a future filled with such love and beauty.
A mirage of deception – I have been knocked down on my ass so many times only to finally get on my feet to start it all over again.

I therefore dust and shake off the dirt and laugh at it --- as if its nothing that is really affecting me.

However, someone always will try to knock me back down. I am ready for them… All I really need is myself to carry me in this life...

Maybe my wounds will eventually heal so it will not open up again.

I will hold my head up high and take a deep breath to shout, "I will not go gently into that good night" but I will rage against the machine, against the scheme's and of course the "dying of the light."

I will make myself feel bigger and stronger than ever before, I will stop feeling scared as soon as I walk out my front door.

## Writer's Block

What blocks your mind? What blocks your idea? Is there some kind of great wall that appears?

Feeling blocked from the world can make things seem so different – making one unbalanced, confused, and bewildered.

I wonder what else can be blocked. What can block the mind or body or soul?

Touch can be blocked... happiness and creativeness too...

What about love or the things that dreams are made of...

Why can't I seem to turn the key... there is something there... I can feel it blocking, blocking... It's deep inside of me...

Small thing... big thing... tick tock, tick tock...

This has got to be important --- I need to step out of the box... down, down the rabbit hole to see how deep this thing can go... Is that the path or is there a different road... I should know but I'm blocked...

Small thing... big thing... tick tock, tick tock...

Smoke and mirrors like the illusions in a magic show... Then there is the smile of the Cheshire cat – ah, the deceiver – this cat I know...

We need to see to believe like we read the words on the page to plant the seeds... the seeds like a person bursting through a pile of leaves... Expressing the love, the need to tell a story... the mind, the creation, the heart and the glory...

So maybe things really can't be blocked... maybe those blocks can be used to build and help things grow... like that special, miracle flower that emerges from the snow...

I continue to write... even if the lock seems too big... I know I will find the key to help my words flow like that river rushing to meet the sea.

The river is wisdom and the ocean is knowledge... They shatter the walls and I will emerge victorious from this deep freeze...

## *You've Got It All*

You know all the right things to say and it makes me wonder... Wonder if you hear what you are saying... you making things too good to be true.

Yeah, you make all these promises but who do you think you are fooling.
I have been working to long... too hard... You must think I am stupid.

Let me get this straight so I do not get this twisted. What in the hell do you really want? What the hell I can give you?

Maybe it is something much more... Because it looks like you want to pimp me out like I am a whore... Nah, that can't be it -- this has got to be some mind-bending trick... I have to be dreaming... please pinch me if I am... cause no noise is coming out yet I feel like I'm screaming...

You seem to think these things are beyond my grasp... it's my imagination you say... Maybe I am crazy, how kind of you to ask...

I feel like I am in a Dr. Seuss book and yes, I would like green eggs and ham.

You've got it all - you think... Well, we shall see whose fooling who and what comes from whom... Can you feel the storm coming? Because I will come knocking, rapping tap, tapping on your chamber door... Are there chills running down your spine from the cracks and creaks in the floor?

I am so tired of all your lies.... Tell me the truth and try to be honest,
I will not get upset.... Really, I promise... I deserve the truth and nothing less, I deserve the truth and I deserve the best.

This is no game, player... I am not a slot machine for you to get bar, bar, bar. All that will get you is lemons sweetie and with those kinds of lemons you will not get very far...

But go on ahead, take peoples gifts, continue to brag... Using folks like you are tucking them into your very own carpet bag...

Well, the secret is out and you know what, you need to find somewhere to hide. The curtain has fallen... the mask is gone... This is the final ride...

You've got it all... maybe... But this façade that you were placating is just an
Illusion of your own making...

I wonder if you hear what you are saying - you making things too good to be true.

## *Addiction*

Good morning, good afternoon or good evening. My name is... Well, my name or the time is really not that important. However, I have a confession to make, I am an addict... yes, I am addicted.

Please understand do not get me wrong, please do not misunderstand...
I am not ready for the benediction... This is a different type of addiction...
Its true -- I do stand and wait in the cold and in the rain...
I travel far to get to it on every occasion... my trip is never the same...
My dealers are different – they are a world apart.
It's amazing but I have so many that I have lost count... I would not even know how to start... I'm addicted its true... But I know what I need to do...

When I get to the place -- you know that place we were before -- they sit me down so I can get me my fix --- I've already paid at the door... I go in knowing this magic carpet ride will help sooth that screaming monkey on my back. And, no its not weed, cocaine or crack.

I am wanting and cravin' this powerful drug. It is not the type you inject in your veins... its deeper... more powerful... it's the spoken word that I crave...

Poetry inspires me to make my own words flow... they are there deep inside you know... Therefore, when it is time for me to come up I will spit my game,

I will do my thing – say what I want to say – I am not the same…

The mike is sanctuary for my addiction… From this sanctuary I spread my message for all to hear… It is not a source of confliction… In this place I am shown respect as my words expose my soul… I am finally free… I am finally home…

Now I do not play and I remember and respect the ones that came before me… The trailblazers – the pioneros - like the NuyoRican Poets *Piri Thomas* and *Pedro Pietri*…

I honor my political and spiritual teachers – my poetic dealers – most especially those of the new school for it is they who took me by the hand, they led me in --- they gave me the tools --- Now I will take this time and share my rhymes --- it is what it is for a reason… I am here – I am now – I am addicted and this is the season… The season of sight through sound – the season of right with might – they mighty pen that is now my sword and I am here -- a warrior women giving praise to the lord because I am addicted…

Trembling - I go off into the cold dark night in search of another venue... Down these mean streets - I need another hit, another fix from my spoken word dealers. Yes, I'm addicted…

# **Sacred Waters**

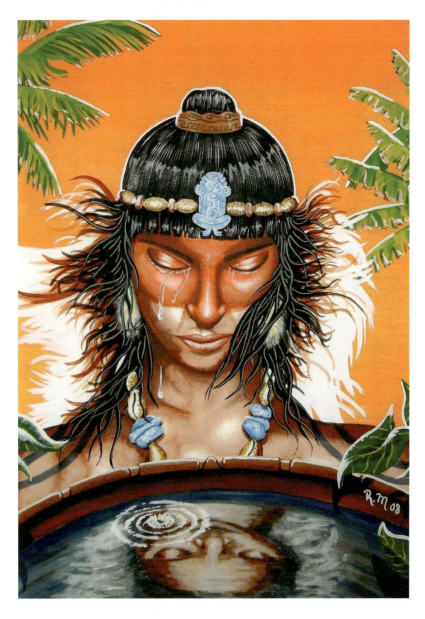

**"Sacred Waters"**
This painting was displayed at the American

Museum of Natural History during a special program entitled "Living in America: Rivers of Life" in January 2008 and at United Nations Headquarters as part of the exhibition "In Celebration of Indigenous Peoples during the Permanent Forum on Indigenous Issues from April 2008 to June 2008. You are invited to interpret it in your own way.

Original size: 20x30 (acrylic)

## *Rain = Cry*

When he was a child my youngest son told me the reason he thought it rained...

He said the rain is really the angels crying for everyone. I was amazed that a child could say such a unique and truly interesting thing.

Since then, I have often thought it should rain everyday just so I can try and better understand a cry... Is crying a special way of cleansing the mind, body and soul? If so why isn't done more often? Is done too much? Like laughter, crying is considered good medicine. I know a good cry can wash away the craziness that is encountered everyday...

I want to cry when I hear people say "rain, rain go away" or "It can't rain all the time." I am thinking maybe it should so it can wash this dirty world clean...

So yes, when it rains it pours... But what is it trying to teach us? It must be an important lesson... At times rain can be destructive... On other occasions it nourishes plant life so these relatives can expose their natural beauty for all to enjoy...

I am thinking to better understand a cry is to see it rain.... Feel it rain.

Just think how rain makes everyone feel... True, it can make you feel sad and blue... But it can soothe the spirit to make you sleepy or come down hard to you wake up... Crying keeps me grounded and close to *Atabei's* – Mother Earth – Mother Ocean's womb... Close enough to hear her heartbeat that soothes...

 I cry when I am happy, sad, frustrated, and confused...

 The way I see -- when I cry it is rain and during those downpours you should be able to see and feel a little of my pain. Maybe this is why I would like it to rain all the time... This way I can try and figure out why no one sees or hears my cry...

## *Sidewalk Memories*

A young girl walks down a sidewalk filled with of all kinds of memories...

This is a path where dreams are created and compiled with all her life's experiences.

She dreams of a life that will either make or break her. Stricken with all of the mistrust and misunderstanding that others have placed upon her; she dreams of having something that could make all of her worries disappear. But these cracks – the ones that break your mamma's back - are turning her dreams into nightmares; her love is coming apart like a jack hammer breaking up a piece of that familiar grey, concrete path upon which she walks and she dreams.

Life and loathing is what he is feeling. He feels disgusted with the cards that he has been dealt; he was hoping for a full house or was it black jack... He is feeling as trapped as if he was in a canvas sack to about to be tossed over a bridge into the East River... He never could keep his feet on the ground...

Back on the sidewalk she is dealing with all the fear, the lies, and the hate... She has been feed and is being led like a donkey following a carrot on a string.
Should she give up walking and sit in the shade? Massage her feet? Call it a day? Should she continue on and on till she gets to the intersection where life meets dreams and victorious themes?

These things she thinks on as she walks down a

sidewalk filled with of all kinds of memories. She moves on with a sigh as if she held some grain of salt and tossed it over her shoulder. Then unexpectedly, she stops to scrape that crewing gum off the bottom of her shoe. She has to get over the hump so she can remove that boulder that has her in a disadvantage.

It is always something and that is a thought that has her frozen in time,
Did she lose her way? Did someone forget to explain that lesson?

As this young girl walks down that sidewalk of memories, she wonders if her decision will make or break her in the end.

## *Goodbye To Lies*

Lies, lies and mores lies is all you ever gave me...

This is why I must say good bye... Good bye to lies and good by to you...

Those lies had me so wrapped up and blind to something right before my eyes, Those lies were so deep they had me lost in a wicked embrace...

It is no wonder why I was feeling like the fox being chased around at a fast pace... You were fully aware that you were in control of everything and cold heart – my love could never change you...

Feeding, deceiving and misleading me like a fool... Abused, I was used like some garage sale tool...

This is why I must say good bye... Good bye to lies and good by to you...

Love you – yes, its insane but I do... However, you think there is no problem... You have no clue... I wonder how you can be this way... I stood by your side while you fed me your lies... I exposed too much of me to you but now what does it matter... The truth is exposed and the light now shines on those dark recesses you call your mind...

There are no excuses... No twisting... No need to try and justify... It's a madness you see for you have become your lie...

This is why I must say good bye... Good bye to lies and good by to you...

I will move on and place this love on a shelf...

You will regress and I can do bad all by myself...

## *What?*

What? I am feeling a little lost and confused with this thing we call life...

Frustrated with this feeling that has positioned itself upon me. It is perched like a raven on a long, cold night... I been disrespected and I don't appreciate it...

Boxed in – it's still dark - and I am just feeling walls unable to get out.

Yelling at the top of my lungs - "I don't want to be lonely anymore!

"Damn it y'all -- can you see the destruction all around?

What? I was not meant to be here at rock bottom looking up for the answer.

Trying so hard to better myself but I'm like that one crab in the barrel being dragged back down so another one can get up on top...

This insanity must stop --- The me, myself and I is at stake here...

Looking at the 'me' through different eyes is what the 'myself and I' must face.

Damn it y'all -- can you see the destruction all around?

What? I do not want to fight anymore,

This sacred garden needs to flourish and grow without the weeds because they are truly choking the life out of me...

Now that I see the grass was never greener on the other side I question...

Whom do I love? What have I done for me lately?
Will I continue to search for something new? Is it really you?
Are these the signs of the times here in the treasure box that has lost its shine?

What? I know all girls want to have fun but love goes that way sometimes...
Should I start dancing on the ceiling and party all night long?
Yelling at the top of my lungs - I don't want to be lonely anymore!

"Damn it y'all -- can you see the destruction all around?

## *Taino Past and Present*

"Taíno Past and Present"

This painting represents what I see as the journey – the past and present, the then with the here and the now. In this piece I feel you can see the best of both worlds - urban village and our ancient Caribbean village. Some things are different but deep down they remain the same. We continue to survive.

I used my son's face as the model in different positions of the face – like the village – the individual over time remains the same. I placed well-known and not so familiar landmarks from New York City within the image.

I wanted to convey that no matter where you are in

time a Taíno is there making a mark in the world and the universe.

Original size: 30x40 (oil and acrylic)

## *The Days Of Old*

Bring back the days of old because the nonsense we have today has me all bored... Yes, I reminisce...

Bring back the old skool hip-hop that made some sense but not these tired rhymes for which I would not pay a red cent.

Why am I so angry about today's music? Well if you need to ask then you are not going to get it anyway... You see I remember Sugar Hill Gang, King Tut $3^{rd}$ and many countless hip-hop artists that I grew up with.... Yeah, bring back the days of old...

Some of the music today can really sounds bad... Not bad as in good but bad as in they shouldn't have... I understand they are trying to make a buck but with any luck they will not end up in jail without bail... Then again who is to say if that might not happen -- then so what -- that's gangsta huh...

I remember the days of break dancing on cardboard boxes at the every street corner. I remember "Planet Rock", "Play at Your Own Risk" used to make every single house party pop... Yeah, bring back the days of old...

Rock Steady Crew, New York City Breakers just name a few, Zulu Nation, DJ Kool Herk were from the Bronx too. Having parties in abandon buildings and hooking it up with the thick electrical wires from the streetlights --- that's how we use to hang and jam all them long hot nights...

Trying --- hoping to get in to see Grand Master Flash spinning the wheels of steel... Enjoying that first jam of the evening that got the whole thing started... "Ya'll want this party started right; y'all want this party started quickly right. Set off -- I suggest y'all, set it off".

Getting comp passes to Roseland, and the Roxy that used to be called 1018's, Latin Quarter's and let us not forget the Garage. Yes, I reminisce... Going to these places put hip hop on the map... The clever clothing like Le' Tigre shirts and those fresh pressed Lee's with the matching Lee jacket with a graffiti tag on the back...

Yeah, I am old school buddy and let's not forget it because it has me feeling ever so young... Man, those were the day when things were so good and everyone had so much fun. We did not have a care in the world... Chillin' at the corner with your closest friends beat boxing and spittin' some hot rhymes, All the while listenin' to "Just Begun", "The Mexican" or "Rock Steady" as time went by. Jammin' to Run Dmc and Jam Master J, LL Cool J and many slamming artist of my day. Man, those ole school jams are still the... Ahhhhh, just thinking about it has me at a point --- yes, I reminisce... Yeah, bring back the days of old...

## Games People Play

Games are things that people play... This is something people say...

The players construct a façade that they hope no one can read...

These players make it difficult for others to love or trust or need...

There are people trying to find that four-leaf clover just to make it through...

It is hard enough trying to get over that hump without the games people do...

Just thinking on the game makes me crazy – these are feelings abused and they makes the vision hazy... hazy as we are looking out over the horizon... spirit risin'... looking for love and crying for help we hope will come from above...

Games are things that people play... This is something people say...

An ongoing battle that happens all the time because the players play and the liars lie... It makes me sad to see – deep feelings dismissed with no regard for a heart's felt wish... Promises given, promises broken like some Chucky Cheese or Dave and Buster token...

I have had my share of tokens -- yes I have been played... Like some tragic circus clown did the big show and will not get paid... I was there unaware that my make-up was running... The player played and his game was so skillful and cunning... So I washed away the clown-face now used... I moving forward with my sight now renewed...

Warrior mode - I am on the lookout for the façade and the mask... Defenses up - I get weary sometimes but I am up to the task... Love is... Love is... Love is... I have also heard it said... I hope to see it some day for I know love is not dead...

So we move, we groove, and still it can be the luck of the draw... A Russian Roulette game with no regard for the law... The universal natural law – reciprocity - that is what the ancients knew... you give to me and I give to you...

Games are things that people play... This is something people say...

Sweet and sour... the hawk swoops down... Chicken Little one day and the next day circus clowns... Fiddle players playing with only one goal... buying auction block slaves in the carnival of souls...

When the spotlight shines... game players scurry like rats running to holes in a life-saving hurry... games affect us all... no matter we are all infected... In our relations and views... in love rejected.

Games are things that people play... This is something people say...

## *Homenaje Spoken*

It wasn't by **Chance** that I took the path that became **True** to me...

The **Majestik** powers that came in like a blue Caribbean wave of vision and poetry... No, I did not **Simply Rob** it to make it my own,
I just fashioned it a little different – you the way a new seed is sown.

I **Blaze-A-Page** with the knowledge that been shared... Getting jiggity like **Papo Swiggity** I am flying high like una **Bella Transtorno** que salo en una forma de poemas... I listen, I learn and my words will excel as move with respect in the territory of the spoken word **Cartel**...

Blessed my ancestors la **Taina** del Caribe hecha de la Isla mas bella de Kiskeia... Testifying scripture like a **Hebrew Mamita...** Brewing potions like **La Bruja** to show off my special little **Magik** tricks like using **Lemon** juice to quench my thirst...

Loving the **Bonafide** poets I'm a most eager pupil following the **Mona Passage** toward the **Nard Truth** like the **Ultimate Boricua** never getting **D-Cross** or **D-Black** from the mission at hand...

**Dr. Loco** fills my prescription and I stay in remission squeezing threw the cracks in this concrete jungle like a **Flaco Navaja** looking toward the **Infinite** possibilities that ride in on the winds of the four directions...

Can you feel my vision? A fusion of the visual and the spoken... That is my **Definition** of poetification because you are never too old to learn and **Advocate Wordz** meant to enlighten... And my aura shines so bright like an **Urban Jibaro** shouting the **Streets-R-Mine** throughout space and time...

As I head **North** to my **Division X** that marks the spot exposing a **Hybrid** that takes a **Rebel Eagle** high in the sky to search for that prize... I'm calling on the **Rain Maker** to baptize me with the words that flow like water and **Broken Silence** so I can **Charan P** these gifts these bestowed... bestowed like **Royal T**.

I am learning to take it nice and slow - can't you see I am that **Chulisi** as I let those whose paths I come across know que yo soy una **Prisonera** de la pintura y la poesia... Asi es **La Roka** que me tiene tan loca...

I am under its **Hipnotic** spell --- I am in a trance that has a strong hold on my soul put the pressure is building as if I was a super **Nova** about to explode.

No es una **Mala Fama** pero el primo de la Luna y Sol...

I am the **G-Positive** to your negative and that makes personal **Jessie Rose** garden bloom...

Vision and poetry... This is my **Soule'** and my passion... It rises in me like a **Taino Soleil** and I am lost and found in this adoration...

It was **SoSoon** that I made it through the door... But I have been blessed to see the best and I am here to share and express as an artist, a woman, and a relative who has her own view from the shore...

Because wasn't by **Chance** that I took the path that became **True** to me.

I pay homage to those who come before me... to those who opened their hearts and minds and shared... Like a long ago *guaitiao*... like relations who care...

You are my inspiration when I paint or when I speak --- like here and now ... This is my homenaje spoken... My special tribute... Cute like me... Loving words and happy and free...

I feel I am home and that is thanks to you...

Therefore I end this homenaje spoken with a big *Bo Matum* and a shout of **CAPICU!**

**Atabei** - Mother Earth

**Bohio** - Home

**Boriken** - Puerto Rico

**Cassava/ Yuka** - Yucca

**Cemi** - Spirits

**Guakia Taino** - We are Taino

**Guakia Yaha** - We are here

**Hamaika** - Jamaica

**Han Han Katu** - So be it

**Itiba Kanubaba** - Bleeding Earth Mother

**Kiskeia** - Dominican Republic

**Kuba** - Cuba

**Makanas** - Weapons

**Okama** - LIsten (Taino)

**Oye** - Listen (spanish)

**Taino** - Noble Ones/ Peasceful people

# Acknowledgements

There's so many that I want to thank that I've met throughout this journey that if I did it would take up at least 7-10 pages really so I'll do my best.

I first would like to thank The Great Creator Jah for blessing me with such awesome parents cause without them I wouldn't be here to share my gift with you all. Their love and support made me the woman you see today. My younger siblings for being there as I began my journey as I venture into the unknown as well as keeping it real. Their words pushed me to go outside the box so I can see life through their eyes. My sons Evan Colon and Nicholas McPherson without you constantly inspiring to be the woman/mother I am today. You guys keep me smiling and laughing when I think life is getting to hard but manage to show me that it's not that serious. I love you both with all my heart and soul. I also would like to thank their father Marvin McPherson for doing such an awesome job in helping and giving me such great advice on my new journey of poetry and paining you're the best.
My homie/co-founder of The W.H.A.T? Show Divino DeNegro, his vision in putting Washington Heights on the map to have so many supporters backing us from the very beginning peace my brother. My art teacher/ business partner Aguilar Marrero, with his knowledge of making such awesome artwork and never said that he was to busy to take the time to teach me how to paint. He's the reason why I'm so determined to be the best I can be so I can share the love of my craft, that I never knew where it would take me. Many various events, fundraiser as well as charity events

we've attended as Taino Spirit. To put it in the words of Juan "PapoSwiggity" Santiago the modern day Frida Khalo and Diego Rivera all because we worked that close together.

I would like to thank Robert "Mukaro" Borrero for taking time out of his busy day to meet with Taino Spirit and giving us the opportunity to showcase our work in places like the Museum of Natural History, VA Hospital in the Bronx and the United Nations Building for the Indigenous forum what an honor to be at all these places. Especially super supportive as I began my journey as a sole poet/artist, being there for me helping me with editing my poems as well as helping me briefly describe each and everyone of my paintings seen in this book. Words cannot express my gratitude towards you for helping me I'm forever in your debt my dear big Natiao love man. George "Urban Jibaro" Torres and Juan "PapoSwiggity" Santiago for believing and pushing me to excel to be the best I can you guys are the best really.  My Ride and Die Girl La Boricua Goddess I especially thank Jah for bringing you into my life. You've  always kept me grounded looking out for me as well listening to me when I feel like the weight of the world is on my shoulder. Being there when things went so sour doing her best to put a smile on my face, showing her loyalty and support when our family with the loss two of the greatest people in the world our parents I truly thank you for that my dear and I truly love you my sister.

Now let me try this in hopes that I can get it ok here I go thank you goes out to the following; Raul Kahayarix Rios, Prisonera Jamas, Sery Colon, Luis Cordero,

Bobby Gonzalez and Maria Aponte-Gonzalez, Luis Benard aka "Nard Truth", David Roberts aka D-Black, Lissette Lissette, Bonfide Rojas, Lemon Andersen aka "Millie's Boy", Taina Brooklyn Poet, Jose Medina of Boricuation, Blaze-A-Page, Mala Fama, Flaco Navaja, Cindy SugaRush, Lah Tere, Rhina Valentin, Vanessa "Hebrew Mamita" Hidry, Peggy Robles-Alvarado, Henry "Ulitmate Boricua" Valentin, Jani Rose, Caridad De La Luz aka "La Bruja", MTK you're the Bomb ma, Jamie "El Masetro" Emeric, Adele Ramos, Abraham Benjamin, Albert "TainoImage" Areizaga, Monica Martinez, Mona Bode, Alica Anabel, The members of El Grito De Poetas, A.B Lugo, Taino Santos, Richard "Ovadose "Santiago and so many of those poets that have supported me throughout my journey and shown be so much love I love y'all so much with all my Heart and Soul really y'all inspired me. You guys already know that if I could actually remember everyone it would take 7-10 pages easy lol.

I can't forget my Futuvision family Rafael Preza and Alexis Sanchez for making me a part if the production Classicos Live "It not a Musical it's a DanceSical", I've enjoyed working on this play. My cast member Edwin Guerrero, Evelyn Escobar, Harold Velasquez and Maggie Rodriguez y'all are so awesome that words can't begin to express my emotion and love I have for y'all.

My dear friends, you know who you are love ya. My peeps from Da Heights 176 Audubon Ave 10033 Zip Code yea all day everyday.

Last but not least my best friend in the whole world

my oldest and dearest friend 3x's Black Belt, Body Guard, Security for most spots throughout the TriState, Shihan Stacy Grayson. You've kept me grounded for years omg I'm forever blessed that you continue to appear when you do and we remained closer then anyone I've ever known. You mean more to me then a friend but more like family love ya man.

Reina M. Miranda aka Sipai'naru (Red Clay Woman) was born in Washington Heights to Dominican immigrant parents who came to the United States like so many others hoping to provide a better life for their children. Reina is the eldest of four and she first found her love of poetry at the age of 18.

Reina has been presenting her spoken word/poetry on the New York City Poetry circuit for over two years. Reina finds her poetic inspiration from the many people she admires and has met at various spoken word events throughout the New York tri-state area. In addition, she uniquely fuses her love of poetry and art with her passion for promoting her Taíno ancestry so she can help others get *"Tainocated"*. This is an educational term used when persons are informing others about the indigenous history of the Caribbean.

In an effort to stay better connected to her Taíno community, Reina is a member of the Cacibajagua Taíno Cultural Society, a group dedicated to promoting Taíno culture via the arts. She is also enrolled with the United Confederation of Taíno People's Taíno Population Census and Inter-Tribal Registry. Reina feels "knowing where you come from will help you get to where you are going".

Sipai'naru - Reina M. Miranda has presented her poetry at some of the following locations:

5C Cultural Club
Capicu Poetry/ Notice Lounge
The NuyoRican Poet's Café
Cemi Underground/ Taino Poetry Night
Nuve's Bar and Café
HOSTOS Community College/ Momma's Hip Hop Kitchen 2
Rebel Art Collective/ S.P.I.T
La Pregunta Café/Feed The Mic
Soule Restaurant/Open Mic Night
Denny Moe's Barbershop/Poetry Under the Tree

For more information or to book Ms. Miranda please visit
[redclaywoman.com](http://redclaywoman.com)